MW01484820

SOF COMBAT CASUALTY CARE HANDBOOK

Foreword

This handbook was previously distributed as a supplement to the *Journal of Special Operations Medicine*. The realm of special operations forces (SOF) medicine is a unique and ever-changing one that demands specialized training for our joint SOF. Managing trauma on today's battlefield presents a dynamic array of challenges where limited resources can be rapidly overwhelmed. An austere environment, hostile gunfire, and delays in casualty evacuation (CASEVAC) are the norms for the special operations medic.

The material in this handbook was gleaned from special operations medics operating in the Global War on Terrorism and other operational environments. It should not be viewed as a substitute for the professional training and judgment of special operations medics; rather, it is designed to be a hip-pocket reference on the tactics, techniques, and procedures (TTP) of SOF-relevant tactical combat casualty care.

Key Lessons

- Ninety percent of combat loss of life occurs before casualties ever reach a military treatment facility (MTF); treatment prior to casualty evacuation is vital.

- Litter carries are fundamental for good patient care; they prevent further injury and get individuals off target as soon as possible. Rehearse manual carry methods prior to deployment.

- Every special operations warfighter should carry a tourniquet and be thoroughly familiar with its application.

- When managing multiple casualties, apply the principles of triage in classifying the priority of treatment and evacuation.

- Rehearse and employ all of the mechanics of CASEVAC from the point of injury to the handover at a MTF.

This handbook provides a number of considerations when employing medical support to SOF in combat. The challenges are numerous, but the special operations medic must deliver medical care to save Soldiers' lives. The collection of TTP in this handbook will enhance the medic's ability to determine the optimum method to deliver casualty survival assistance.

Steven Mains
Colonel, Armor
Director
Center for Army Lessons Learned

Chapter 1

Special Operations Forces Combat Casualty Care

Introduction

Managing combat trauma on the modern battlefield represents challenges that are scarcely encountered within the civilian community. The advent of tactical combat casualty care (TCCC) represented a fundamental paradigm shift from the care of casualties (CAX) that evolved in the late 1970s. Special operations forces (SOF) engaged in combat operations, removed from conventional forces (CF) and with austere logistical support, represent a set of unique challenges, as well. The limited amount of equipment and medical supplies, coupled with delays in evacuation, add to what is already a frightening experience. Being wounded also generates great fear and anxiety in the CAX. Special operations medics, exposed to hostile fire while caring for CAX, become likely targets, resulting in the special operations medic unintentionally becoming "part of the problem, not the solution" and forcing CAX to care for themselves. The conditions associated with this type of environment demand specialized training for all SOF. We refer to this specialized training as SOF combat casualty care.

Historical Perspective

The foundations of SOF combat casualty care began with the Advanced Trauma Life Support (ATLS) Training Program. ATLS was established after a tragic plane crash in 1976 in rural Nebraska, which devastated an entire family. The pilot, an orthopedic surgeon, was seriously injured, while his wife was killed instantly. Three of his four children sustained critical injuries. This physician had to flag down a passing motorist to transport his children to the nearest hospital. Upon arrival, he found the small rural hospital locked. Even after the hospital was opened and a physician was called in, he found the emergency care provided at the regional hospital inadequate and often inappropriate. Once he returned to work, the physician, with assistance from advanced cardiac life support (ACLS) personnel and the Lincoln Medical Education Foundation, began to collate a set of protocols for the management of such patients and produced the initial framework for the national ATLS course. These protocols were adopted by the American College of Surgeons (ACS) Committee on Trauma (COT) in 1980.

The original intentions of the ATLS courses, modeled on the ACLS program, were to train physicians and nurses who did not manage trauma routinely in the initial management of the severely injured patient. Several changes in the standard protocols used to treat trauma CAX were modified. Previously, a complete evaluation was performed; a diagnosis was made; and only then, was the casualty treated. The new approach was to establish a protocol to assess then treat the most life-threatening injuries first, and accordingly, move on to the next injury. The "ABCs" of trauma was established to prioritize the order of assessment and treatment. Nothing new was added; current evaluation procedures were simply reorganized to reduce morbidity and mortality in the "golden hour" of trauma. The ATLS pilot courses were introduced in Auburn, Nebraska in 1977. By 1980, these courses expanded nationally under the auspices of the ACS. Early reports on the implementation and evaluation of these pilot courses and the improvements in civilian trauma care appeared in the literature soon afterward.

Since that time, ATLS has been accepted as the standard of care for the first hour of trauma management and taught to both military and civilian providers. In 1981, shortly after the development of the ATLS course, the ACS/COT and the National Association of Emergency Medical Technicians entered into a cooperative agreement to develop an ATLS course for prehospital providers. This course was appropriately named Prehospital Trauma Life Support (PHTLS). The first PHTLS course was taught in New Orleans in 1984. PHTLS is nationally endorsed and widely adopted as a continuing educational program by hospitals, educational institutions, emergency medical service agencies, and military medical programs and is incorporated into many initial and refresher emergency medical technician/emergency medical technician–paramedic courses.

Until recently, U.S military medical personnel were trained to care for combat CAX using the principles put forth in the ATLS model. The inappropriateness of many of these measures when applied to combat CAX initiated the TCCC project by the U.S. Naval Special Warfare Command and was continued by the United States Special Operations Command (USSOCOM). USSOCOM developed a new set of tactically appropriate battlefield trauma management guidelines in 1996. These guidelines focus primarily on the most common causes of preventable death on the battlefield and the most protective measures that can be reasonably performed in combat, taking the special operations tactical environment and the unique patterns and types of wounds into consideration while developing casualty management recommendations.

TCCC guidelines, used in special operations since 1998, have proven successful in combat operations. In 2001, USSOCOM recognized the need to update these guidelines, and based on research conducted by the Naval Operational Medical Institute, a Committee on Tactical Combat Casualty Care (CoTCCC) was established. This committee updated the TCCC guidelines in 2003 and republished them in the revised PHTLS manual, 5th edition.

CoTCCC is an ongoing project conducted under the sponsorship of the Navy Bureau of Medicine and Surgery. The unique aspect of this joint organization is that it includes special operations personnel, including special forces medics, Navy SEAL corpsmen, Air Force pararescuemen, trauma surgeons, emergency medicine physicians, anesthesiologists, and medical educators, who collaborate to continually update TCCC guidelines. TCCC was established as the standard of care for special operations medic training in 2005. TCCC equipment and training also became mandatory for all deploying SOF, as the first responder to a wounded special operations warfighter on the battlefield is often not a special operations medic. Since World War II and the war in Vietnam much of the decline of combatants killed in action (KIA) can be attributed to TCCC training, techniques, and equipment.

SOF Combat Casualty Care

SOF combat casualty care applies to all special operations components and the full range of military operations involving the integration of special operations assets conducting special and irregular operations in a joint, combined, or multinational environment. SOF combat casualty care is the medical management provided to CAX in a tactical, combat environment. This medical management is often in contrast to CF, with its robust logistics tail, its focus on stabilizing the casualty, and the rapid rearward movement capability to advanced hospital trauma care.

There are many dynamic factors on the modern battlefield that may influence combat casualty care including the following:

- Enemy fire: This may prevent the immediate management of CAX at the point of injury (POI) or wounding and may place the combat lifesaver (CLS)/medical personnel at risk while providing care to CAX.

- Medical equipment limitations: CLS/medical personnel are generally limited to what they are carrying in their CLS kit or medical aid bag.

- A widely variable evacuation time: In the civilian community, evacuation is generally under 25 minutes; in a combat situation, it may be delayed for several hours.

- Tactical considerations: Tactical constraints that may take precedence over medical care and the timely evacuation of CAX.

- Casualty transportation: CASEVAC may or may not be available. Air superiority must be achieved before any air evacuation assets will be deployed. As stated previously, the tactical situation must dictate when or if CASEVAC can occur. Additionally, there are environmental factors that may prevent evacuation assets from reaching CAX.

Note: The ongoing and evolving process to standardize terminology is evident when using the terms medical evacuation (MEDEVAC) and casualty evacuation (CASEVAC) within the CF and joint SOF arena. The Army Medical Department (AMEDD) uses the term MEDEVAC when referring to the evacuation of CAX using dedicated, standardized medical evacuation platforms, with medical personnel providing en route care. CASEVAC, according to the AMEDD, is reserved for casualty evacuation by non-medical vehicles, watercraft, or aircraft, with or without en route medical attendance. In the SOF arena, evacuation of CAX will often be accomplished by other than dedicated U.S. Army aeromedical or special operations forces aircraft. U.S. Air Force (USAF) may also perform this extraction of the team and CAX. USAF reserves the term MEDEVAC for the aeromedical evacuation of stable patients from one medical treatment facility (MTF) to another.

SOF are advised to avoid the term MEDEVAC when discussing the initial management of combat CAX and use the term CASEVAC instead to eliminate any misunderstanding of the mission required. This publication will use the term CASEVAC throughout to denote the evacuation of CAX by ground vehicle, watercraft, or aircraft assets.

The force health protection (FHP) of SOF requires an enhanced medical capability to reduce preventable deaths and minimize effects from injuries. The following are some of the aspects that make SOF combat casualty care unique:

- The combat CAX may not be a U.S. military asset; in fact, the CAX may not be uniformed military at all. This is particularly true within the U.S. Army Special Forces operational environment where host nation personnel may be among the wounded.

- The special operations unit may be operating in remote, denied areas, far forward of any CF or supporting medical infrastructure; i.e., beyond normal logistical lines, with a limited and difficult resupply of essential medical items or evacuation capabilities.

- Evacuation time to an Echelon II MTF may be prolonged due to the mission, enemy, terrain and weather, troops and support available, time available, and civil considerations.

- Tactical considerations (clandestine or low-visibility operations) or the depth of penetration into the hostile environment by the special operations unit may make CASEVAC unfeasible.

- The priority focus of special operations air assets remain insertion, extraction, and resupply of special operations assets. Historically, CASEVAC missions have been "lifts of opportunity."

The unique medical capabilities of SOF directly contribute to the likelihood of special operations mission accomplishment and force sustainment.

Trauma on the battlefield

Statistics reflect that up to 90% of combat loss of life occurs before CAX ever reach an MTF. For this reason, management at the POI or wounding prior to CASEVAC is vital. Statistics also reveal that the KIA rate in Operation Iraqi Freedom (OIF) and Operation Enduring Freedom (OEF) (12.5%) is half of what it was in World War II (25.3%) and a third less than Vietnam and Desert Shield/Storm (18.6%).

CAX with uncontrolled hemorrhage compose the largest group of potentially preventable deaths on the battlefield. Statistically, the deaths that occur on today's battlefield result from the following:

- Penetrating traumatic brain injury (TBI). Most of these cases are not survivable, and these CAX are triaged as expectant.

- Surgically-uncorrectable torso trauma. Trauma to this region has significantly decreased due in part to the use of Interceptor Body Armor/Improved Outer Tactical Vest; however, trauma to unprotected areas, such as the axillary region, still occurs and is frequently not survivable. Penetrating wounds to the abdomen, without significant vascular involvement, may be survivable for several hours.

- Potentially correctable surgical trauma.

- Exsanguination; hemorrhage from extremity wounds remains the leading cause of preventable death. Extremity wounds account for over 60% of all wounds on today's battlefield.

- Mutilating blast trauma. These horrific wounds are not usually survivable. Improvised explosive devices (IEDs)/vehicle-borne IEDs (VBIEDs) are the leading cause of morbidity and mortality in OIF/OEF.

- Tension pneumothorax (PTX). This is the second leading cause of death on the battlefield. Penetrating chest trauma still exists, even with the advent of body armor, and can become rapidly fatal without timely medical intervention.

- Airway obstruction/injury; the third leading cause of preventable death. While this is a small percentage, mostly due to maxillofacial trauma, these injuries require immediate attention to ensure survivability of CAX.

- Died of wounds, mainly due to infection and shock.

The primary types of wounds caused by weapons are penetrating, blast, and thermal trauma. Unlike the civilian community where the majority of wounds (70%) are blunt trauma in nature, usually from motor vehicle crashes, the majority of wounds in combat are caused by penetrating injuries from bullets (23%), shrapnel injuries (62%), and blast injuries (3%). Secondary debris is also frequently associated with these types of penetrating wounds.

Note: IEDs/VBIEDs have caused about half of all American CAX in OIF and about 30% of combat CAX in OEF, both KIA and wounded in action.

Exsanguination, PTX, and airway obstruction/injuries are significant because they are potentially avoidable with appropriate medical management and intervention using SOF combat casualty care principles and techniques. In fact, it is estimated that of all preventable deaths, 90% might be avoided with the simple application of a tourniquet for extremity hemorrhage, rapid management of a PTX, and the establishment of a viable airway.

Stages of Care

SOF combat casualty care is designed and structured to meet three important goals: manage CAX, prevent additional CAX, and complete the mission. In SOF combat casualty care, the management of CAX that occurs during combat operations is divided into three distinct phases, each with its own characteristics and limiting factors:

- **Care under fire**: The care rendered by the special operations warfighter, CLS, or special operations medic at the POI while they and CAX are still under effective hostile fire. Available medical equipment is limited to that carried by the individual warfighter, CLS, or special operations medic in their medical aid bag.

- **Tactical field care**: The care rendered by the CLS/special operations medic once they and CAX are no longer under effective hostile fire. Tactical field care also applies to situations in which an injury has occurred, but there is no hostile fire. Available medical equipment is still limited to that carried into the field by medical personnel. Time to evacuation from the POI or other casualty evacuation point to an MTF may vary considerably, from a few minutes to many hours.

- **Combat CASEVAC care**: The care rendered once CAX have been picked up by an aircraft, vehicle, or boat and transported to a higher level (echelon) of care. Additional medical personnel and equipment may have been pre-staged and made available at this stage of casualty management.

Chapter 2

Care Under Fire

This stage of special operations forces (SOF) combat casualty care denotes the care rendered by the special operations warfighter, combat lifesaver, or special operations medic at the point of injury (POI) while they remain under effective hostile fire. The risk of additional casualties (CAX) at any moment is extremely high for both the CAX and medical personnel; optimally, controlling the tactical situation is the key to saving the lives of the CAX.

The major considerations during this stage of care include:

- **The suppression of hostile fire**: The best management of CAX may entail the special operations medic moving with the fire team and providing effective, suppressive return fire. Ultimately, the tactical situation must dictate when and how much care the special operations medic can provide. Finally, when a casualty evacuation (CASEVAC) is requested, the tactical situation may not safely allow the air asset to respond. Remember in the care under fire phase, the treatment of CAX involve a combination of good medicine and good tactics.

- **Moving the casualty to a safe position**: When under effective enemy fire, the special operations medic (whether mounted or dismounted) cannot afford to rush blindly into the kill zone/danger area to provide interventions of questionable value to rescue a fallen comrade. Medical personnel are limited, and if injured, no other medical personnel will be available until the time of evacuation during the CASEVAC phase.

Control of hemorrhage is vitally important as trauma involving major vasculature may rapidly result in hypovolemic (hemorrhagic) shock; non-life-threatening hemorrhage should be ignored at this time. Again, extremity hemorrhage is the leading cause of preventable death on the battlefield. Use of temporary tourniquets, such as the Combat Application Tourniquet, SOF Tactical Tourniquet, or improvised devices to control bleeding is essential in these injuries. If the CAX need to be moved, a tourniquet is the most reasonable initial technique to control major hemorrhaging and may allow CAX to continue the fight. Ischemic damage to the extremity is rare if the tourniquet is applied and left in place for less than one hour; in fact, tourniquets have been applied for 4-6 hours without deleterious effects. Israel Defense Forces reported over 90 cases of tourniquet application and found complications only after 150 minutes, none of which resulted in the loss of the injured limb. Again, management of non-life-threatening hemorrhage while under effective hostile fire should not be attempted and should be deferred until the tactical field care phase.

Control of hemorrhage in non-extremity wounds may best be accomplished by the tried-and-true method of direct pressure using an Emergency Trauma Dressing or a combination of Kerlix packing and Ace bandages. If the hemorrhage site is accessible, hemostatic agents such as the HemCon, QuickClot, or Celox bandages, in conjunction with direct pressure, are more effective at achieving external hemostasis. Severe hemorrhage may also be the result of trauma to the neck, axillary, or groin area. Trauma of this nature is not amenable to the use of tourniquets; however, direct pressure and the use of hemostatic agents may be effective in bringing this type of hemorrhage under control.

Note: As CAX may exsanguinate before medical help can arrive at the POI, guidelines that are more liberal have been established for the use of a tourniquet to control severe external hemorrhage from an extremity. As the presence of hypovolemic (hemorrhagic) shock is a grave prognostic sign, every special operations warfighter should carry a tourniquet and be thoroughly familiar with its application.

Potential hazards of time and exposure to enemy fire do not warrant the application of a cervical collar for stabilization of the cervical spine prior to moving CAX to cover, particularly if they have sustained only penetrating trauma. Other neck injuries such as those resulting from a fall from 15 feet or more, fast-roping injuries, parachuting, or motor vehicle accidents may require cervical spine stabilization unless the danger of hostile fire constitutes a greater threat. In this case, cervical spine stabilization and long spine board immobilization will be a secondary consideration to moving CAX to cover.

In cases of blunt trauma, the risk of spinal cord injury from neck movement must be weighed against the risk of continued exposure to effective enemy fire. Studies have determined that only 1.4% of CAX with penetrating trauma might have benefited from cervical spine stabilization. Special operations medics should carry an adjustable rigid cervical collar in their medical aid bag. If rigid cervical collars are not available, a SAM Splint or a rolled blanket may be used as a field expedient collar. A long spine board is generally not available; however, there are many materials available in urban environments (door, bed frame, etc.) that may be used to achieve rudimentary spinal immobilization.

Determine the potential risks associated with moving forward to a casualty's position:

- Did the casualty result from a detonated mine or booby trap?

- Did the casualty result from an improvised explosive device (IED) or vehicle-borne IED? IEDs have been used to draw U.S. Soldiers into a coordinated, follow-on ambush or have subsequently triggered pre-placed, secondary explosives to kill medical responders and bystanders.

- Consider available assets; will the continued application of firepower outweigh any attempt to recover/transport the casualty at this time?

Once you determine that moving CAX is warranted, standard litters are usually not available for moving CAX in the care under fire phase. Consider using alternative methods for evacuating them (short versus long distances):

- Short distances:

  ° Dragging CAX out of the field of fire by web gear, uniform, or even a length of rope attached to a snap link.

- ° Manual carries (one/two-person drag, poncho drag, firefighter's carry, etc.).

- Long distances: Commercial litters such as the SKED stretcher, Talon IIC, or Foxtrot may be available, especially if the unit is mounted. Improvised litters, such as discarded doors, bed frames, or other material may also be utilized.

If these items are not readily available, and the risk of hostile fire injury to CAX requires immediate retrieval, CAX may be grasped by the shoulders of their uniforms, their heads stabilized by the forearms, and dragged along the ground to cover.

Chapter 3

Tactical Field Care

The tactical field care phase of special operations forces (SOF) combat casualty care is distinguished from the care under fire phase by the increased time available to provide medical care and a reduced level of hazard from hostile fire. This term also applies to situations where an injury has occurred while conducting an operation, but the injury was not a result of hostile action. This phase of care is characterized by:

- A reduced risk of exposure to hostile fire (risk has not been completely eliminated).

- Medical equipment that has been carried into the field by the special operations medic and other special operations warfighters on infiltration.

- The highly variable time available for managing casualties (CAX). In many cases, tactical field care may consist of a cursory evaluation and rapid management of wounds, with the expectation of re-engagement of hostile fire at any time. In other cases, there may be ample time to perform a more thorough evaluation and to render whatever care is available in the field.

Once the tactical situation is under control and/or CAX have been recovered and moved behind cover, the special operations medic should initiate triage (in the case of multiple CAX) and manage all CAX. In this phase of care, a more in-depth evaluation and management of CAX, reassessment of conditions and interventions previously performed, and a focused approach on the conditions not addressed during the care under fire phase may be initiated. However, management of CAX must still be dictated by the tactical situation at hand. Nonessential evaluation and management of CAX must be avoided during this time. Care must be rendered once the mission has reached an anticipated evacuation point, without pursuit, awaiting casualty evacuation (CASEVAC); however, the special operations medic should take great care to allocate his medical supplies and equipment in the event re-engagement of enemy action occurs or the evacuation is delayed.

Place CAX in the coma position (recovery position), optimally with their head at the same level as their heart. If hypovolemic (hemorrhagic) shock is a possibility, elevate their feet 6-8 inches (modified Trendelenberg position).

Note: The special operations medic should not abandon the basic principles of body substance isolation while caring for CAX. Even under battlefield conditions, wear gloves (latex or vinyl) and protective glasses, as a minimum, not only to protect against contact with serological fluids, but also to keep your hands clean. Blood and fluids are slippery, and if you do not don gloves and your hands become bloody, it is difficult to clean them in the field. You will end up wiping your bloody hands on your uniform and cross-contaminating other CAX.

Establish priorities

Obtain situational awareness, contain the scene, and assess CAX.

Form a general impression

If no other warfighter was present at the time of the injury, briefly note any clues as to the mechanism of injury to develop an index of suspicion as to the underlying trauma and organ systems that may be involved, as the signs and symptoms may be subtle. For instance, the presence of hearing loss (possible tympanic membrane rupture) as a result of blast injury should alert the special operations medic to the possibility of blast injury to internal organs (gastrointestinal, lungs). Note the casualty's body position, overall appearance, and any outward signs of distress.

Cardiopulmonary resuscitation

If CAX of a blast or penetrating trauma are found to be without a pulse, respirations, or other signs of life, do not initiate cardiopulmonary resuscitation (CPR). Attempts to resuscitate a traumatic cardiopulmonary arrest (TCPA), even in urban settings in close proximity to a trauma center, have rarely been successful. Despite a rapid and effective prehospital and trauma center response, CAX with prehospital cardiac arrest due to trauma rarely survive. TCPA CAX with the best outcome are generally young, have treatable penetrating injuries, have received early (prehospital) endotracheal intubation, and have undergone prompt transport (typically ≤10 minutes) to a trauma care facility. TCPA in the field due to blunt trauma is fatal in all age groups. On the battlefield, the cost of attempting CPR on trauma-induced cardiac arrest CAX may be measured in the additional lives lost as care is focused on these CAX and withheld from other, more survivable CAX.

Note: CPR should only be considered in the case of non-traumatic disorders, such as hypothermia, near drowning, or electrocution.

Assess the level of consciousness

Fix the casualty's gross level of consciousness (LOC) and mental status using the acronym "AVPU" (casualty is **a**wake and **a**lert, responds to **v**erbal stimuli, responds to **p**ain, or is **u**nresponsive). Determine if the casualty is alert and oriented to person, place, time, and preceding events (A&O x 1, 2, 3, 4).

Note: The four main reasons for an altered LOC are traumatic brain injury (TBI), pain, shock, and analgesic medications (e.g., morphine).

As stated previously, any casualty with an altered LOC should be disarmed (weapons and grenades) as a precautionary measure, lest they "mistake the good guys for the bad guys."

Airway management

Conscious, spontaneously breathing CAX require no immediate airway interventions. If the casualty is able to speak normally, the upper airway is intact. As a rule, required interventions should proceed from the least invasive procedures to the most invasive. Do not attempt any of these maneuvers if CAX are conscious and breathing adequately on their own. Allow them to assume a position that is the most comfortable, facilitates breathing, and protects their airway. In this phase of care, this may include a semi-sitting (Fowler's) position or sitting upright.

If CAX are unconscious, the likely cause is hypovolemic shock or possible TBI; in either case, they cannot protect their own airways adequately. With unconscious CAX that are not exhibiting signs of airway obstruction, open their airways using the chin-lift or trauma jaw-thrust maneuvers as appropriate. Assess the airway by listening and feeling for air movement. As in the care under fire phase, cervical spine stabilization is generally not required, except in the case of significant blunt force trauma.

If spontaneous respirations are present without respiratory distress, an adequate airway in obtunded or unconscious CAX is best maintained with a 28 FR nasopharyngeal airway (NPA). An NPA is preferred over an oropharyngel airway (OPA) because it is better tolerated in the casualty who has an active gag reflex and/or regains consciousness. The NPA is also preferred over the OPA because it is less likely to dislodge during casualty movement. Once the NPA has been inserted, place the casualty in the coma-position to maintain an open airway and to prevent aspiration of blood, mucous, or vomitus.

Note: Remember, insertion of an NPA is contraindicated in the presence of or a suspected basilar skull fracture.

Note: Many times proper positioning alone may be all that is required to maintain a viable airway; however, CAX should be moved as little as possible to assess the airway when trauma above the clavicles is present. CAX with maxillofacial trauma should never be transported lying supine on litters. If they need a more definitive airway, a blind insertion airway device (BIAD), such as the Esophageal-Tracheal Combitube or King LT should be your next choice. These dual-lumen devices are easily inserted and are able to maintain an open airway better than a simple NPA.

Note: Traditionally, the endotracheal tube (ETT) has been the "gold standard" for airway support due to its isolation of the trachea, permitting complete airway control. However, under combat conditions, the ETT has several disadvantages:

- Inserting the ETT is a far more perishable skill, if not practiced routinely.

- Inserting the ETT entails the use of (tactically unsound) white light on the battlefield.

- Accidental esophageal intubations are much less likely to be recognized under combat conditions and may result in fatalities.

- Even under optimal conditions, 30% of attempts at endotracheal intubation by civilian emergency medical technician-paramedic personnel are unsuccessful.

For CAX with a present or impending airway obstruction, again the initial intervention is to open the airway using the chin-lift or trauma jaw-thrust maneuvers, as appropriate. These maneuvers should be followed by the insertion of an NPA; however, if an airway obstruction develops or persists despite the use of an NPA or BIAD, a more definitive airway is indicated. Significant airway obstruction in the combat setting is likely the result of penetrating wounds of the face or neck. In cases where blood obscures facial landmarks or the maxillofacial trauma has grossly distorted or destroyed anatomical features, an emergency surgical cricothyrotomy may be indicated. This procedure should also be considered in the presence of airway edema (inhalation burns, inhaled toxic fumes) that may prevent traditional intubation.

Although an emergency surgical cricothyrotomy is typically only used after failed attempts at oral intubation, it may be appropriate to consider this the next step when an NPA or BIAD is not effective. As stated, this technique is also appropriate in the case of substantial maxillofacial trauma where blood or disrupted anatomy precludes the use of other airway adjuncts. The insertion of a large-bore cannula or ETT through the easily identifiable cricothyroid membrane is faster than intubation, allows rapid access to the airway for ventilation, and is safe and effective in trauma CAX. In the hands of a properly trained special operations medic, this emergency procedure may be the only viable alternative when other airway devices are not effective. An emergency surgical cricothyrotomy can be performed, under a local anesthetic, on a casualty who is conscious and/or has an active gag reflex. This procedure is not without hazards and as with any surgical technique, it is a perishable skill that requires routine practice.

Note: If an emergency surgical airway is performed or BIAD inserted, it is not a procedure you can perform and forget. The special operations medic should assign another warfighter to continually monitor these CAX. It may also be necessary to use a bag-valve-mask (BVM) device to ventilate them if their respiratory rate drops below 8 breaths/minute or exceeds 24 breaths/minute. Once again, if CAX are moved or logrolled, they must be reassessed to ensure the airway adjuncts have not become dislodged.

Note: Oxygen (O^2) is usually not available during this phase of care because the cylinders of compressed gas and the associated O^2 equipment are too heavy and bulky to be carried by the special operations medic; however, consider its use as it becomes available (CASEVAC care phase).

Breathing

Assess breathing by first inspecting the casualty's chest. Open the body armor and shirt and inspect for deformities, contusions, abrasions, penetrations, burns, lacerations, and swelling (DCAP-BLS) and an equal, bilateral rise and fall during respirations. Briefly note the breathing rate and quality. Palpate both the anterior and posterior of the chest, feeling for tenderness, instability, and crepitus. Anteriorly, this is a rapid and systematic palpation from the top of the clavicles to the lower margin of the ribcage using your open and spread hands and fingers. Posteriorly, this is a systematic blood sweep looking for additional or exit wounds.

Note: The use of auscultation in this setting is not appropriate; it is doubtful you will be able to use your stethoscope in the noisy and chaotic battlefield environment.

Traumatic chest wall defects may result in a tension pneumothorax (PTX). A tension PTX occurs when a one-way valve is created, usually by a penetrating wound, where air cannot escape the pleural space and unilateral pressure builds within the pleural space. A tension PTX may also occur with the application of an occlusive dressing over an open PTX. This type defect should be managed quickly by sealing the defect, both entrance and exit (ideally during expiration), with an occlusive dressing without regard to "venting" one of the four sides of the dressing, as this is difficult to maintain in a combat setting. Be certain to fully expose CAX to observe for other chest wall defects or exit wounds. A petrolatum (Vaseline) dressing, battle dressing, or tape may be used. An Asherman Chest Seal is also an effective device for this purpose. The CAX should also be placed in a sitting/semi-sitting position and should be monitored for the development of a tension PTX.

Assume any casualty with signs and symptoms of progressive, severe respiratory distress on the battlefield, resulting from unilateral penetrating chest trauma, to be a tension PTX. Do not rely on typical (clinically-observed) signs, such as unilateral decrease/absence of breath sounds, tracheal deviation, unexplained hypotension, and hyperresonance (hypertympanic) to percussion over the affected side, as definitive indications of a tension PTX, as these signs may not always be present even though a tension PTX exists. Since these signs may be difficult to ascertain under battlefield conditions, your index of suspicion should be presumptive, based on the presence of penetrating chest trauma and the progressive signs/symptoms of respiratory distress indicating the need for chest decompression. Chest decompression is accomplished in this setting using a 14-gauge (angiocath-type) catheter-over-needle (needle thoracentesis).

Note: Most CAX will have some degree of hemo/pneumothorax resulting from penetrating chest trauma. The additional trauma associated with a needle thoracentesis is unlikely to significantly exacerbate injuries, even in the absence of a developing tension PTX. As stated previously, a tension PTX is the second leading cause of preventable death in combat.

Decompression of the chest is performed by introducing the 14-gauge, 2½-3-inch needle catheter through the second intercostal space at a 90-degree angle at the mid-clavicular line over the top of the rib, into the pleural space on the affected side. Once the needle catheter has been properly inserted, the needle is removed, leaving the catheter in place. Although it may be difficult to appreciate under battlefield conditions, a "rush" of air should be elicited with proper insertion technique. If there is no "hissing" sound of escaping air once the needle is inserted, then it was not inserted deeply enough, or a tension PTX was (is) not present.

Reassess CAX for decreased signs/symptoms (if conscious) of respiratory distress. Tape the catheter in place, as a recurrence of a tension PTX is likely. Apply a securing bandage or small dressing and continually monitor CAX as catheters used for this procedure are subject to "kinking" or becoming occluded with blood. Place CAX in a sitting position to provide some level of comfort and make it easier for them to breathe.

Note: Chest tubes (thoracostomy) are not recommended during this phase of care as they are not necessary for the initial management of a tension PTX, and this technically difficult and more time-consuming procedure has little documented advantage over a needle thoracentesis in relieving a tension PTX. Additional tissue damage, complications, and subsequent infection are also less likely with a needle thoracentesis versus a chest tube thoracostomy. Studies have also indicated that chest tubes without suction capability have been unsuccessful in re-expanding lungs with a PTX following penetrating chest trauma.

Circulation and hemorrhage control

Reassess any tourniquets applied in the care under fire phase; quickly perform a gross visual inspection of casualty's anterior and manage any significant bleeding found. Beginning at the casualty's head and moving towards his feet, perform a "blood sweep" of the entire posterior, inspecting and palpating for any significant hemorrhage not already addressed. Reassess any interventions already performed and manage any life-threatening bleeding as rapidly as possible, using tourniquets (Combat Application Tourniquet, SOF Tactical Tourniquet) for extremity hemorrhage as necessary/appropriate.

Once CAX have been transported to the casualty evacuation point where CASEVAC is anticipated, reassess any tourniquets previously applied. It may be possible to remove the emplaced tourniquet and utilize direct pressure, elevation, pressure dressings, and/or hemostatic agents; however, do not hesitate to reapply a tourniquet to control hemorrhage and ensure continued hemostasis. However, you must complete any required fluid resuscitation prior to tourniquet removal. It may not be necessary to completely remove the tourniquet, only to loosen it. This will allow the tourniquet to be reapplied if the hemorrhage cannot be controlled using other methods. It is important to remember, once CAX are resuscitated and their systolic blood pressure (BP) rises towards normal, bleeding may resume through the tourniquets. Monitor the tourniquet(s) and tighten as necessary.

Note: During your assessment, remove the absolute minimum of clothing necessary to expose and manage injuries. If conditions dictate, expose, examine, and re-cover CAX because of time constraints, tactical requirements, and to protect them from the environment.

Traumatic amputations

Amputations have become more common with the continued enemy use of improvised explosive devices and vehicle-borne explosive devices. In the event of a traumatic amputation, you must first stop the bleeding. Once this has been accomplished by the use of a tourniquet or pressure dressing, cover the stump to further control bleeding and protect the open wound. A Kerlix dressing and a 6-inch Ace wrap are effective for this purpose.

If the tactical situation permits and there are no other CAX, collect the amputated limb, rinse free of debris (normal saline, Lactated Ringers), and wrap the appendage loosely in saline-moistened sterile gauze. Seal the part in a plastic bag or cravat. If an air asset evacuates the casualty, it may be possible to place the amputated part in a cool container; however, do not allow the part to come in direct contact with the ice or allow it to freeze. Even if the amputated limb cannot be reattached, skin from it may be used for grafting to cover the limb end.

Resuscitation indicators

Assess perfusion by evaluating the casualty's skin color, condition, and temperature. Normal skin should be pink, warm, and either dry or moist to the touch. Skin that is pale and cool to the touch may indicate hypoperfusion; cyanosis is indicative of tissue hypoxia.

The BP is commonly used to determine the need for fluid resuscitation; however, stethoscopes and BP cuffs are rarely available or useful to the special operations medic on the noisy and chaotic battlefield. A rapid method of determining the casualty's state of perfusion is to palpate various pulses to note if they are present. Checking for the strongest palpable pulse is important when considering the casualty's circulatory status and is especially helpful to assist in determining if the casualty is a candidate for continued fluid administration. For reference purposes:

- A palpable radial pulse represents a systolic pressure of at least 80 milliliters of mercury (mmHg).

- A palpable femoral pulse represents a systolic pressure of at least 70 mmHg.

- A palpable carotid pulse represents a systolic pressure of at least 60 mmHg.

Note: CAX should only be resuscitated to a systolic BP of 80 mmHg; this level is adequate to perfuse all vital organs, but not so high as to initiate re-bleeding of a vessel that has already clotted. Re-bleeding can occur at BP readings as low as 93 mmHg (systolic).

As previously discussed, do not attempt to resuscitate TCPA CAX on the battlefield. If, however, they have significant blood loss and a weak radial pulse or are not coherent and have not suffered TBI, once external bleeding is controlled, intravenous (IV) fluid resuscitation should be initiated.

Vascular access

Not all CAX injured in combat require IV fluid resuscitation; however, when tactically feasible, all significantly injured CAX should have at least a saline lock initiated in anticipation of the possible subsequent administration of IV fluids, analgesics, or antibiotics (ATB).

The use of a single 18-gauge catheter-over-needle is preferred in the tactical field setting because of the ease of cannulation, which conserves the special operations medic's supplies. The 18-gauge catheter is considered adequate for the rapid delivery of crystalloid and colloid resuscitative fluids and emergency medications. Blood and blood substitute products (Hemopure, Polyheme) require larger catheters and are generally not administered in this phase of care.

Note: IV access should not be attempted on an extremity that has a fracture or a significant wound proximal to the insertion site. Cleaning the venipuncture site with an antimicrobial solution prior to inserting a catheter is optional under emergency conditions.

If peripheral IV insertion is problematic, avoid using the internal jugular or subclavian vein because of the potential complications associated with central lines. The saphenous or external jugular veins are alternatives that are more appropriate; however, intraosseous (IO) infusion is the best alternative when IV insertion is unsuccessful. Fluids and medications delivered by IO infusion are administered at the same dose that would be given intravenously.

The algorithm for fluid resuscitation in the tactical environment is guided by the presence of a palpable radial pulse and normal mental status (mentation) in the casualty. Both are adequate and tactically relevant resuscitation indicators to either initiate or withhold fluid resuscitation, and both can be adequately assessed in noisy and chaotic environments without mechanical devices.

While early IV access should be obtained for CAX with significant injuries, only those CAX who exhibit signs of hypoperfusion (defined by absent peripheral pulses or altered mentation) and who have not suffered a TBI are given fluids. If CAX have only superficial wounds, intravenous fluid resuscitation is not necessary. In the absence of abdominal wounds or nausea, the administration of oral fluids should be encouraged. It is likely blood loss has ceased, even if CAX have significant wounds, if there are no obvious signs of bleeding or shock and CAX are coherent. In these cases, establish IV access, but hold fluids at this time. Reevaluate the casualty as frequently as possible. These CAX should have a single saline lock initiated with an 18-gauge catheter; remember, a single access portal is sufficient and serves to conserve supplies and time.

As stated previously, when IV access is difficult or the tactical situation intrudes, modern IO fluid delivery systems, such as the (sternal IO) First Access for Shock and Trauma (F.A.S.T.1), are reasonable substitutes for peripheral IV access and are a major improvement over the "venous cutdown" which are time-consuming, technically difficult, and require instrumentation. IO infusion has been a reliable method for achieving vascular access and infusing fluids and blood for many years. In addition to the F.A.S.T.1 system, the Bone Injection Gun and the Vidacare EZ-IO system have been found useful when existing methods of vascular access are challenging or impossible.

Note: Sternal IO access is not recommended if the casualty is a child or an adult of small stature (less than 50 kilograms [kg]), has a fractured manubrium/sternum, or has significant tissue damage at the site. IO devices are considered short-term devices and, optimally, should not be left in place for more than 24 hours.

Fluid resuscitation depends on the amount, both weight and volume, of fluid that can be carried by each special operations medic (or team cross-loaded) and the characteristics intrinsic to the fluid itself. Mission constraints will dictate how much fluid is available on the battlefield. Special operations medics should infuse 500 milliliters (ml) of Hetastarch (Hextend) after external hemorrhage has been brought under control (direct pressure, tourniquet). Another 500 ml of Hextend may be infused if there is no response; infusion of Hextend should not exceed 1,000 ml or 20ml/kg/h.

Hextend is an FDA-approved, balanced electrolyte solution that resembles the composition of the principal ionic constitutes of normal plasma. Hextend is a formulation of 6% Hetastarch, combined with physiologically balanced electrolytes, a lactate buffer, and physiological levels of glucose. One 1,000 ml bag of Lactated Ringers, one hour after infusion, will expand the intravascular fluid volume by approximately 250 ml. One 500 ml bag of Hextend will expand the intravascular fluid volume by approximately 800 ml in a similar time period. One 500 ml bag of Hextend is functionally equivalent to three 1,000 ml bags of Lactated Ringers; this expansion is sustained for at least eight hours.

Hextend is typically administered via an installed saline lock. The saline lock is a plastic male adapter with a rubber hub at one end and a tapered plastic tip at the other that is inserted directly into an IV catheter, secured to the catheter, and taped (or secured with a Raptor IV band) over the venipuncture site to prevent displacement. The lock is flushed with 2.0 ml of normal saline; flushing with additional saline is also required periodically (at least every two hours). Fluids are administered by inserting an 18-gauge, 1¼-inch needle/needle-catheter (attached to the fluid administration tubing) through the (cleansed) lock. The catheter is left in place and secured with tape or a circumferential Velcro wrap (Linebacker) to prevent it from becoming dislodged. The flow capabilities are 30 ml/min by gravity feed, 125 ml/min utilizing pressure infusion, and 250 ml/min using syringe-forced infusion.

Fluid resuscitation algorithm

The rate of fluid administration is based on the casualty's hemodynamic status and whether or not hemorrhage has been controlled. When managing superficial wounds (typically > 50% of injured), no immediate intravenous fluids are required; again, oral fluids should be encouraged in the absence of abdominal wounds or nausea.

If the casualty is coherent and has a palpable radial pulse, blood loss from a significant extremity or torso wound, with or without hypotension, has likely ceased. Initiate a saline lock, withhold fluids at this time, and reevaluate them as frequently as the tactical situation will allow. If appropriate, have the casualty sip small quantities of water to assist hydration status.

If the casualty is not coherent and has no palpable pulse with significant blood loss—stop the bleeding using whatever means (previously discussed) at your disposal. Many hypotensive CAX suffer from torso wounds, unaffected by your resuscitative measures (CAX may have lost as much as 1,500 ml or as much as 30% of their circulating blood volume). Once hemorrhage has been controlled to the extent possible:

- ~~Initiate intravenous access and administer 500 ml Hextend (via the saline lock) at a max rate of 20ml/kg/h.~~

- If mentation improves and a palpable radial pulse returns, discontinue the fluids and flush and maintain the saline lock.

- If there is no improvement in mentation and radial pulses are not palpable, administer a second 500 ml of the Hextend and continue to monitor pulses and LOC.

- If no response is seen after 1,000 ml of the Hextend has been infused, you may need to consider conserving your supplies and turning your attention to other, more salvageable CAX.

Note: ~~Remember, a liter of Hextend is functionally equivalent to more than 6 liters of Lactated Ringers solution.~~ If a casualty's pulse is not palpable after infusing a liter of Hextend, he is likely continuing to hemorrhage internally (third space); this casualty will only benefit from rapid evacuation to a definitive (surgical) medical treatment facility. Continued large doses of fluids will have a transient effect on the

CENTER FOR ARMY LESSONS LEARNED

casualty's BP but will also dilute his blood's ability to clot; this will actually cause the wounds to hemorrhage more freely. Infuse sufficient fluids to perfuse the vital organs, but not enough to promote continued hemorrhage.

TBI and head injuries are special situations; hypotension and hypoxia exacerbate secondary brain injury and are difficult to control in the initial phases of SOF combat casualty care. If the casualty is conscious and has no peripheral pulse, resuscitate to restore a palpable (radial) pulse and evacuate as soon as possible for more definitive (surgical) care.

Dress all wounds to prevent further contamination and to facilitate hemostasis. The Emergency Trauma Dressing or "Israeli Bandage," that consolidates a primary dressing, pressure applicator, secondary dressing, and closure apparatus, is ideal for this purpose. Check for additional wounds/exit wounds since the high velocity projectiles from modern assault rifles may tumble and take an erratic course when traveling through tissues or when striking bone. These type projectiles may create exit wounds that may be quite remote from the entry wound. Again, only remove the clothing necessary to expose and manage wounds. Care must be taken to prevent CAX from developing hypothermia.

Prevention of hypothermia

Combat trauma CAX have a high percentage of penetrating injuries with variable evacuation times. These CAX are at a high risk for hypothermia, which is defined as a whole body temperature below 95° Fahrenheit (F). Mortality has been twice as high (53%) in CAX with a core body temperature less than 89°F, as compared with CAX with a core body temperature less than 93°F, which may result in a 28% mortality rate.

Hypothermia can occur regardless of the ambient temperature. The blood loss typically associated with combat trauma results in a peripheral vasoconstriction, contributing to the development of hypothermia. The longer CAX are exposed to the environment during trauma management and evacuation, the more likely it is that hypothermia will ensue. This is even more likely during CASEVAC using rotary-wing assets.

Hypothermia, acidosis, and coagulopathy constitute a vicious cycle in trauma CAX. When these three elements are present, the casualty's blood clotting mechanisms are inhibited. The absolute need to monitor and prevent hypothermia is highlighted by the fact that up to 10% of combat CAX arriving at Level III treatment facilities exhibit some degree of hypothermia. During the tactical field care phase, the special operations medic must first minimize the casualty's exposure to the elements. If possible, maintain all protective gear on CAX; however, try to replace any wet clothing. As always, prevention remains the best method to counter hypothermia.

Prior to evacuation, CAX must be wrapped in dry blankets, ponchos, etc. to prevent heat loss during transport, even if the temperature is 120°F. Ideally, they should be maintained as close to a normal body temperature (normothermic) as possible. Special operations medics should carry Ready-Heat or the Hypothermia Prevention and Management Kit (HPMK). The HPMK Blizzard Rescue Blanket, Thermolite Hypothermia Prevention System Cap actively warms to 110-118°F once it is applied.

In cold environments, ensure IV fluids are warmed prior to administering to CAX. Using the Thermal Angel Blood and IV Fluid Infusion Warmer or meals, ready to eat heaters on either side of a fluid bag will help to warm the fluids.

Pneumatic Anti-Shock Garment (PASG)

The PASG may be available in mobility or evacuation assets during the CASEVAC care phase and may be useful for pelvic stabilization and the control of pelvic and abdominal bleeding, as these areas are outside of the area protected by Interceptor Body Armor/Improved Outer Tactical Vest. The application and extended use of the PASG require careful monitoring. The use of this device is contraindicated with penetrating thoracic injuries, suspected traumatic disruption of the diaphragm, and TBI.

Note: Once applied, do not remove the PASG until CAX are in a location where the underlying injuries can be surgically repaired. Premature deflation of the PASG can result in sudden and profound hypotension.

Monitoring and continued evaluation

During the tactical field care phase, continue to monitor CAX clinically and provide reassurance until evacuation is possible. Indirect measure of the O^2 saturation of the peripheral tissues may be assessed using a pulse oximetry (ultra-portable) device (as an adjunct). The following ranges are supplied solely as a reference:

- Normal range: 95-99% SpO^2 (continue to monitor).

- Mild hypoxia: 91-94% SpO^2 (provide O^2 if it becomes available).

- Moderate hypoxia: 86-90% SpO^2 (provide 100% O^2 if it becomes available).

- Severe hypoxia: < 85% SpO^2 (100% O^2 and ventilate by BVM).

Note: Remember, pulse oximetry readings may be misleading in certain settings:

- Cold extremities or hypothermia may cause falsely low SpO^2 readings.

- Shock (hypoperfusive states) and when peripheral circulation is impaired and arterial pulsations in the limbs are diminished make accurate readings difficult.

- Anemia or carbon monoxide poisoning can displace O^2, saturate hemoglobin, and result in falsely high SpO^2 readings.

Carefully recheck all interventions performed. Inspect and dress all wounds.

Pain management

All CAX in pain should be provided analgesia; recognize that CAX will handle pain in their own way. Logically, the type, amount, and route of administration (orally versus intravenously versus intramuscularly) of the analgesic given will depend on the casualty's status and the severity of the pain. It is easier to prevent pain than to have them "suck it up" and have to manage them once it has become too much for them to bear.

If CAX are lucid and otherwise capable of lending their firepower to the fight, pain medications should be administered orally (PO). This will not immediately alter the casualty's LOC and he will be able to join in the fight, increasing the survivability of the team. The recommended medications for these CAX are Meloxicam (Mobic) 15 milligram [mg] PO qd along with acetaminophen (Tylenol) 650 mg (bi-layered caplets), two PO q8h.

These two medications along with an oral ATB will constitute the "combat wound pill pack" that each special operations warfighter should carry. Each pill pack should include instructions to take all medications contained within the pack if they sustain a penetrating wound on the battlefield, except in the case of abdominal wounds.

Note: Special operations warfighters should avoid taking any aspirin products while operating in a combat area because of their interference with platelet function and detrimental effects on the body's ability to form a clot and halt both internal and external hemorrhage.

If the casualty is seriously injured, in pain, and otherwise unable to fight, he should be provided narcotic analgesics. Closely monitor these CAX for the signs/symptoms of respiratory depression that are inherent with many narcotics. Clearly and visibly document the use of any narcotics to avoid accidental overdose and respiratory compromise. If the casualty is without IV or IO access, administer:

- An oral transmucosal fentanyl citrate (OTFC), 400-800 microgram [mcg] PO transmucosally, lozenge stick ("lollipop") placed in the casualty's mouth between the cheek and lower gum. It is recommended to tape the spent lozenge to their finger to avoid accidental overdosing. Reassess the casualty q15min and repeat the dose once if necessary to control pain.

- Alternately, Intranasal Ketamine may be administered for non-injectable pain management.

If the CAX has IV or IO access, administer Morphine sulfate (MSO4), 5 mg (initial dose) slow IV push; dose can be repeated q10 minutes, titrated to effect.

Note: Morphine administered IV has an immediate onset with a peak onset of approximately 20 minutes; administered intramuscularly (IM), morphine's onset will be within 15-30 minutes with a peak onset of 30-60 minutes. Accompany MSO4 use with promethazine (Phenergan), 25 mg IV, IO, or IM q4h, for synergistic analgesic effect and for controlling the nausea that often accompanies morphine administration.

Note: Remember, the contraindications for MSO4 use include unconsciousness, hypovolemic shock with a decreased LOC, head injuries, and respiratory distress.

If a saline lock is used to administer these medications, the lock should be flushed with 5 ml of saline following the MSO4 administration. Again, you must ensure there is some visible indication of the time and amount of morphine given and document it on the casualty's DD 1380 Field Medical Card (FMC).

Note: Special operations medics must always have naloxone hydrochloride (Narcan) on hand when administering any narcotic. This narcotic antagonist can quickly reverse the effects of opiates if necessary. An initial dose of 0.4 mg to 2.0 mg IV push, repeated at 2-3 minute intervals for a maximum of 10 mg as required. Naloxone is a shorter-acting medication than morphine, so repeat doses are often necessary.

Fracture management

Inspect and palpate all extremities (DCAP-BLS/tenderness, instability, and crepitus) and splint all fractures (the joint above and the joint below the injury) as circumstances allow, ensuring that peripheral pulses, motor, and sensory checks of the extremity are performed before and immediately after splinting materials are applied. If there is a decrease in distal pulses following the application of a splint, simple adjustments of the splint usually remedies the problem. If after adjustments are made and distal pulses remain absent, slight repositioning of the extremity toward the normal position of function may reinstate circulation. Make certain you remove and secure any restrictive items CAX may be wearing such as rings or watches prior to evacuation.

Note: Humeral and tibial/fibular fractures can account for 500-750 ml estimated blood loss (EBL); femoral fractures may account for up to 1,500 ml EBL. A traction device (splint) may be available if the SOF are mounted and should be applied to both open and closed femoral fractures as its application may slow bleeding and alleviate pain significantly.

Application of splinting materials may prevent further harm by immobilizing the underlying bone. The special operations medic cannot rule out a fracture by physical examination in the field. Severe sprains and strains can present signs/symptoms identical to a fracture; therefore, when in doubt, splint it if time and the tactical situation allows. Remember: Life over limb always.

Infection control

Infection remains an important cause of morbidity and mortality on the modern battlefield, and the special operations medic must assume that all penetrating wounds on the battlefield are infected and manage them accordingly. Broad-spectrum ATBs are indicated for the management of these contaminated wounds. The factors the special operations medic must take into account when selecting the appropriate ATB are the route of administration and any medication allergies CAX may have.

- If CAX are conscious and able to take oral medications, a 400 mg tablet of gatifloxacin (Tequin, Zymar), taken once daily, is recommended. Alternately, moxifloxicin (Vigamox) 400 mg tablet, taken once daily may be substituted.

Note: Currently, gatifloxacin is contained in the "combat wound pill pack" issued to each warfighter. CAX should take this and all medications found in the pack as

soon as they receive a penetrating wound, except abdominal wounds, after all
life-threatening injuries have been addressed.

- If CAX are unconscious, in shock, or otherwise unable to take oral
  medications, the ATB should be administered IV or IM. The
  recommended ATB for these CAX with penetrating wounds are cefotetan
  (Cefotan), 2 grams (g) administered IV, over 3-5 minutes or IM, q12h or,
  alternately, ertapenem (Invanz), 1 g IV, over 30 minutes or IM, q24h.

Note: CAX with a preexisting hypersensitivity to penicillins should not receive
cefotetan due to the cross-sensitivity between cephalosporins and penicillins.
Ertapenem 1g is diluted with 3.2 ml of 1% lidocaine (Xylocaine), without
epinephrine when administered intramuscularly.

Communication

While performing assessments and interventions on the casualty, the special
operations medic should be constantly talking to and reassuring the casualty.
Combat is already a frightening experience, and being wounded generates
tremendous anxiety and fear of death or gross disfigurement. Engaging the casualty
with reassurance and explaining what you are doing before you do it (as tactically
feasible) can be immensely therapeutic.

Recheck the casualty's airway, breathing, and circulation every few minutes and
after every intervention to ensure they are "still with you."

Evacuation decision

Once all life-threatening injuries have been addressed, pain and ATB medications
have been administered, and any other "loose ends" have been tied up, the special
operations medic must determine the casualty's evacuation priority, and the
casualty must be packaged for transport. When managing multiple CAX, apply the
principles of triage in classifying the priority of treatment and evacuation.

While the evacuation category decision must be based on the casualty's present
medical condition, tactical constraints must also be taken into consideration. In the
SOF arena, the tactical compromise inherent in rotary wing aircraft may interfere
with timely evacuation. Other factors, such as mission, enemy, terrain and weather,
troops and support, time available, and civil consideration and the availability of
evacuation assets, may reflect the ability or inability to evacuate CAX to the next
level (echelon) of care.

The decision to evacuate by CASEVAC should be made as early as possible.
Waiting to call in these air assets may delay definitive medical care and result in a
bad outcome for CAX. Request the CASEVAC, or have another warfighter
accomplish it for you, using the standard nine-line request procedures format.

While conducting deep operations or when the theater is not sufficiently developed
to allow conventional forces aeromedical evacuation assets to be used effectively,
the primary means of evacuation by air will be by special operations aviation assets.
It is essential that pre-mission coordination be made through the theater special
operations command for flight medics or pararescuemen to accompany the flight
when backhauling CAX. Otherwise, the special operations medic may be required

to accompany CAX in order to provide en route medical care, possibly leaving warfighters on the ground without proper medical support. Communication between the special operations medic and CASEVAC personnel is critical to good casualty handover.

Documentation

Document your clinical assessments, interventions performed, and changes in the casualty's status utilizing the DD Form 1380, FMC. Ensure these cards are firmly attached to CAX and forwarded to the next level (echelon) of care. If an FMC is not readily available, use 3-inch white tape to record pertinent data (written with indelible ink) and affix it to the casualty's chest.

Chapter 4

Casualty Evacuation Care

Medical management of combat casualties (CAX) during the previous phases of care is provided in settings that are sometimes hostile but always austere, with the nearest medical treatment facility (MTF) minutes, hours, or even days away. However, at some point in the operation, special operations forces (SOF) will be recovered onto an aircraft, watercraft, or other ground asset for extraction. In some circumstances, the special operations warfighters and CAX will be extracted together.

Planning for the evacuation of CAX will often require synchronization with conventional forces (CF) for air and/or ground assets. Generally when special operations assets are conducting operations in support of CF, the special operations command and control element is the focal point for this effort.

As special operations assets function with a limited medical support infrastructure, detailed pre-planning and coordination for casualty evacuation (CASEVAC) and leveraging CF capabilities are vital. Elements of a viable, synchronized, and mutually understood CASEVAC plan must include:

- Planned and reconnoitered evacuation routes (operational environment considerations).

- Identified aeromedical launch requirements and hasty landing zones that support the mission.

- A robust and interoperable primary, alternate, contingency, and emergency communications plan.

- Liberal use of non-standard CASEVAC platforms.

- CASEVAC transfer points and/or projected receiving MTF.

- Thorough dissemination and rehearsal of the CASEVAC plan to all SOF and CF (down to the lowest level).

Combat CASEVAC care is the care rendered once CAX have been placed aboard the aircraft, boat, or vehicle for transport to a higher level (echelon) of care. Generally speaking, combat CASEVAC care is a continuation of the care that was initiated during the tactical field care phase, with some notable enhancements:

- Additional medically-trained personnel may accompany the evacuation asset(s). This is important for several reasons: The special operations medic may be among the CAX; there may be multiple CAX that exceed the special operations medic's capability to manage simultaneously; and the additional medical personnel, such as physicians or other specialists, may provide greater on-site expertise.

- Additional medical equipment may be available at this stage of casualty management. This equipment may be pre-staged prior to infiltration of the team. Medical resupply may also be accomplished during the CASEVAC phase.

More advanced medical equipment such as blood, blood substitutes (oxygen-transporting fluids), other fluids, and oxygen (O^2) may become available with the arrival of these evacuation assets. A full set of vital signs may be accomplished at this point. Electronic systems capable of monitoring the casualty's blood pressure (BP), heart rate, pulse oximetry, and end-tidal carbon dioxide detectors may now be available and should be leveraged. Typically, this equipment and the improved environment within the evacuation asset allow for more advanced and definitive management of CAX.

During this phase of care, CAX must be reassessed for an effective airway, adequate breathing, and control of hemorrhage. Temporary tourniquets may be replaced with pressure dressings or hemostatic agents; intravenous (IV) lines may be initiated. IV fluids in this phase may include whole blood, O-positive or O-negative packed red blood cells (PRBC), or blood substitutes. The need for further analgesia should be assessed and administered as necessary.

Airway management

Airway management during the CASEVAC care phase follows the identical principles discussed during the tactical field care phase:

- Opening of the airway using the chin-lift or jaw-thrust maneuvers, positioning CAX, and the use of a nasopharyngeal airway (NPA) are still the initial management techniques of maintaining an effective airway.

- An emergency surgical cricothrotomy remains an appropriate option when an NPA is not effective. If the casualty is conscious, lidocaine 1% should be used during this procedure.

- If conditions allow, and the proper equipment is available, endotracheal intubation is a viable option in the CASEVAC care phase. Again, the Esophageal-Tracheal Combitube (ETC) and the King LT are the recommended options for securing the airway, as these devices can be inserted without the need for illuminated laryngoscopy (many tactical aircraft have restrictions on the use of illumination within the aircraft during combat operations). Either of these devices may produce adequate ventilation and, in the case of the ETC, protect the airway from aspiration.

- Endotracheal intubation is a viable option if the use of white light is not prohibited by the tactical circumstances.

Note: Laryngoscopy and endotracheal intubation require skills that must be performed on a frequent basis to remain proficient. While special operations medics receive training in the use of the endotracheal tube (ETT), they use it infrequently. Unfortunately, special operations medics may not be able to use the laryngoscope or may be unable to place the ETT. For this reason, the ETC and King LT are useful alternatives. If none of these airways is feasible, the emergency surgical cricothyrotomy remains an option. Regardless of the airway device, refresher training must take place on a frequent basis.

Breathing assessment

As with airway management, assessment of the adequacy of breathing in the CASEVAC care phase is a continuation of the interventions performed during the tactical field care phase. Continue to assess any penetrating chest wall defects and the interventions previously performed. Monitor for the development of a tension pneumothorax (PTX). If the casualty has unilateral penetrating chest trauma and progressive respiratory distress, manage the existing or developing tension PTX with:

- Occlusive (4-sided) dressing materials (Vaseline-impregnated gauze, tape, or a field dressing).

- Decompression (needle thoracentesis).

- A chest tube (thoracostomy) with Heimlich valve attached. This procedure should be considered if no improvement with needle decompression or when a long transport is anticipated.

Note: For CAX who show no improvement with needle decompression, the special operations medic should suspect a tension hemo/pneumothorax may be present.

- Administer O^2 (when available) if lowered SpO_2 via pulse oximetry, casualty is unconscious, suspected traumatic brain injury (TBI), possible hypoperfusion (shock) may ensue, or the casualty is to be transported at altitude.

Control of hemorrhage

Assess CAX for any previously unrecognized hemorrhage. Control the hemorrhage (as appropriate) using:

- Direct pressure, combined with elevation (extremity).

- Pressure dressings (Emergency Trauma Dressing, Kerlix, Ace wrap).

- Tourniquets (Combat Application Tourniquet, SOF Tactical Tourniquet, improvised).

- Hemostatic agents (HemCon, QuickClot, Celox).

Assess CAX for the possibility of removing tourniquets once bleeding has been controlled by other means. Remember, this may only be done once the special operations medic has completed any required fluid resuscitation and positive response(s) to resuscitation efforts are seen:

- Peripheral pulses that are normal in character.

- Normal mental status checks.

Do not hesitate to reapply the tourniquet to control hemorrhage and to ensure continued hemostasis.

IV access; fluid resuscitation

Reassess CAX for hypovolemic (hemorrhagic) shock:

- Altered mentation, in the absence of a TBI.

- Abnormal vital signs trending (elevated pulses, increased respirations, skin cool to the touch, possible hypotension).

Initiate IV access (install a saline lock) if not already done. If IV access is not obtainable, initiate venous access by intraosseous (IO) route.

If resuscitative fluids are deemed necessary, guided by a weak or absent radial pulse and abnormal mentation:

- Administer 500 ml of Hextend, IV bolus.

- Administer an additional 500 ml Hextend IV, if signs of shock are assessed. Do not administer more than 1,000 ml of Hextend under these conditions.

If the casualty has a palpable radial pulse and a normal mental status:

- Withhold IV fluid administration at this time.

- Provide fluids orally (PO) if conscious (and no abdominal wound or nausea is present).

- Continue to monitor the casualty.

If a casualty with an isolated TBI is unconscious and has a weak or absent radial pulse, resuscitate as necessary to maintain a systolic BP of 90 mmHg or above, unless the TBI is concurrent with hypovolemic (hemorrhagic) shock. In this case, the special operations medic should resuscitate the casualty as he would any other shock casualty.

Transfusions

Traumatic injuries may cause massive bleeding resulting in rapid loss of O^2-carrying capacity. Generally speaking, there is little reason to transfuse blood or blood products in the field if the bleeding can be stopped. However, if there is a significant evacuation delay, transfusion of fresh whole blood (FWB), PRBC, blood components, or blood substitute (O^2-transporting) products may be a viable option.

Transfusion of blood under MTF conditions is not without risks, and obtaining fresh blood from one warfighter for immediate transfusion to another warfighter under austere field conditions requires safeguards that are even more stringent.

As the storing of blood and blood products is difficult from a logistics point of view, special operations medics have long relied on a standard pool of "walking blood bank" donors, composed of previously typed special operations warfighters. To eliminate the need for donor blood typing in the field, the special operations medic should also identify the blood Type-O warfighters for emergency FWB transfusions.

Hypothermia prevention

As previously stated, the special operations medic must strive to maintain CAX in a normothermic state. Remember, prevention of hypothermia is as important as any other resuscitation effort.

Monitoring

Continue to monitor vital signs and pulse oximetry and continue to provide O^2 to CAX (as necessary). As often as possible and every time CAX are moved, the special operations medic should reassess all interventions performed to include:

- Airway maintenance (airway adjuncts emplaced).

- Chest trauma management (occlusive dressings, invasive procedures performed including needle thoracentesis or chest tube thoracotomy).

- Perfusion status (need for additional fluids or need for withholding fluids and signs or symptoms of IV infiltration or malfunction).

Wounds and fractures

Check to ensure hemostasis and efficacy of tourniquets applied, hemostatic agents, and/or dressings applied. Check for additional wounds that may have been missed and reassess wounds that have already been addressed. Continue to ensure the casualty is not developing hypothermia.

Reinspect extremities and splint all fractures if not already done, ensuring that peripheral pulse, motor, and sensory checks of the extremities are performed before and immediately after splinting materials are applied. If not already done, remove and secure any restrictive items the casualty may be wearing (ring, watch).

Inspect the pnematic anti-shock garment (if applied) to ensure it has not become damaged or deflated. Ensure stopcocks are secured in the closed position. Continue to monitor the device, ensuring the pumping mechanism remains attached to the garment during transport.

The special operations medic should not initiate debridement of the wounds during transport of CAX. The conditions aboard the aircraft, watercraft, or vehicle (darkness, instability, contamination) make such efforts inadvisable. Debridement of assault rifle wounds has been shown to be of less benefit to wound healing than previously thought. In any event, these procedures are best deferred until arrival at the MTF.

Pain management

If the casualty has sustained a penetrating wound, remains lucid, and has not already done so, have him take all medications contained in his combat wound pill pack. Again, these recommended medications are meloxicam (Mobic) 15 mg PO qd along with acetaminophen (Tylenol) 650 mg (bi-layered caplets), two PO q8h.

If narcotic analgesics are indicated and the casualty is without IV or IO access, administer:

- OTFC lollipop, 400-800 mcg PO.

- Alternately, the Intranasal Ketamine may be administered.

Note: Remember, the special operations medic must clearly and visibly document the use of narcotics to avoid accidental overdose and respiratory compromise. Naloxone (Narcan) must be readily available whenever administering narcotics.

If narcotic analgesics are indicated and the casualty has IV or IO access, administer:

- MSO4, 5 mg (initial dose) slow IV push; dose can be repeated q10 minutes, titrated to effect.

- Promethazine (Phenergan), 25 mg IV, IO, or intramuscularly (IM) q4h.

Antibiotics

As previously addressed, antibiotics are recommended for all penetrating combat wounds.

If able to take PO medications:

- A 400 mg tablet of gatifloxacin (Tequin, Zymar), taken once daily, is recommended.

- Alternately, moxifloxicin (Vigamox) 400 mg tablet, taken once daily, may be substituted.

If unable to take PO medications (unconscious, shock):

- Cefotetan (Cefotan), 2 grams (g) administered IV, over 3-5 minutes or IM, q12h.

- Alternately, ertapenem (Invanz), 1 g IV, over 30 minutes or IM, q24h; diluted with 3.2ml of 1% lidocaine (without epinephrine) when administered IM.

Note: Remember, CAX with a preexisting hypersensitivity to penicillins should not receive cefotetan due to the cross-sensitivity between cephalosporins and penicillins.

Documentation

Remember to document clinical assessments, interventions performed, and changes in the casualty's status on their field medical card (FMC). Again, ensure the FMC (or 3-inch white tape) is securely attached to CAX during transport.

Evacuation

Coordinate evacuation based on the casualty's precedence: critical (urgent), priority, or routine.

Note: Although CASEVAC operations in Iraq and, to a lesser extent, in Afghanistan are conducted at relatively low and insignificantly changing altitudes, CASEVAC missions may involve altitudes that are clinically relevant. These changes must be taken into consideration by the special operations medic anytime a casualty or item of medical equipment that contains a "trapped" quantity of air is used. CAX with closed or PTX that will be transported through significant altitude changes (greater than 500 feet), should have the closed PTX converted to an open PTX (needle thoracentesis). If a casualty has been intubated with a cuffed tube and subsequently ascends to a significantly higher altitude, the cuff will attempt to expand by the same proportion as the reduction in ambient air pressure. This may result in significant tracheal injury. Conversely, if the casualty subsequently descends in altitude, the cuff will shrink in size due to the increasing ambient pressure and will lose its seal and security in the casualty's airway. A technique is to inflate the cuff using sterile saline; however, it requires less liquid to properly inflate the cuff.

Appendix A

Combat Triage

Overview

Triage is a French word meaning "picking, sorting, or choice" and is derived from the Latin *tria* meaning three; the term literally means sorting into three categories. In common terms, triage is a method of dealing with the following conflicting factors:

- Number, location, and severity of the injury(ies).

- Time constraints (severity of injuries may not allow time-intensive procedures to be applied, for example, cardio-pulmonary resuscitation).

- Tactical situation.

- Overall mission or operation.

- Availability of medically-trained assistance; combat lifesaver and self-aid/buddy-aid.

- Availability of evacuation assets with regard to time, distance, and terrain.

- Medical re-supply capabilities and requirements.

- Likely outcome of the individual casualty must be factored into the decision process prior to committing the limited resources.

Triage ensures the limited medical resources available to the special operations medic are used to provide care for the greatest benefit to the largest number of casualties; i.e., afford the greatest number of casualties the greatest chance for survival. Triage is a dynamic process and decisions are made at every stage in the movement of the casualty.

While performing triage, the special operations medic will be responsible for balancing human lives against the realities of the tactical situation, the level of medical resources on hand, and the realistic likelihood of the casualties' survival. The decision to withhold care from a casualty who in another less overwhelming situation might be salvaged is a difficult one for any medical professional. However, this is the essence of triage. Fortunately, decisions of this nature are infrequent even in mass casualty situations.

The traditional categories of triage are immediate, delayed, minimal, and expectant. An additional category of urgent has been used to describe casualties that are surgical candidates.

Appendix B

Casualty Evacuation Operations

Medical evacuation (MEDEVAC) is the timely, efficient movement and en route care by medical personnel of wounded, injured, or ill casualties (CAX) from the battlefield to a medical treatment facility. Evacuation begins when medical personnel receive the injured or ill warfighter and continues as far rearward as the casualty's medical condition warrants or the military situation requires. If dedicated medical vehicles, boats, or aircraft are available, CAX should be evacuated on these conveyances to ensure they receive en route medical management. For special operations forces purposes, casualty evacuation (CASEVAC) refers to casualty evacuation by medical or non-medical vehicles or aircraft, with or without en route medical attendance.

Special operations assets operating in the field have limited force health protection (FHP) resources and are often dependent upon the theater FHP infrastructure for the majority of their health care requirements at Level II and above. FHP planning for operations where the risk of penetrating trauma is high requires extensive planning and coordination with conventional forces. Special operations medical planners should ensure CASEVAC operations are addressed in the operations plan (OPLAN)/operations order (OPORD) as a separate operation, as these operations require significant preplanning and coordination. Communications and procedural issues must be synchronized to ensure timely evacuation from the battlefield. The OPLAN/OPORD should also determine requirements for the MEDEVAC of host nation/coalition military, and civilians and the protocols and procedures involved.

The same format used to request aeromedical evacuation (air assets) is used for requesting ground and waterborne evacuation.

Nine-Line CASEVAC Request Format	
Line 1	Location of the extraction site
Line 2	Radio (FM) frequency and call sign/suffix
Line 3	Number of CAX by precedence
Line 4	Special equipment required
Line 5	Number of CAX by type
Line 6	Security of extraction site
Line 7	Method of marking the extraction site
Line 8	Nationality and status of CAX
Line 9	Nuclear, biological, and chemical (NBC) contamination

The senior special operations medic present should make the determination to request CASEVAC and assign precedence. The decision is based not only on the condition of the CAX, but also on the tactical situation. The precedence assigned to CAX provides the supporting CASEVAC unit and controlling headquarters with:

- Information that will be used in determining priorities for committing their evacuation assets.

- Validated information to ensure resources will not be unduly strained.

- Casualty classification. CAX with the greatest need (highest classification) are evacuated first and receive the necessary care required to help ensure their survival (the tendency to over-classify a wound remains a continuing problem). Brevity codes should be used in accordance with Field Manual (FM) 8-10-6, *Evacuation Request Procedures*, to prepare all CASEVAC requests. Brevity codes should also be listed in the signal operating instructions (Automated Net Control Device [ANCD]). These requests are transmitted by secure means only, typically using the Single-Channel Ground and Airborne Radio System. The use of nonsecure communications dictates that the request be transmitted in an encrypted form. The only information on the CASEVAC request that is not encrypted (transmitted in clear text) is the call sign and suffix (Line 2).

Give the following in the clear: "I have a CASEVAC request," and wait 1 to 3 seconds for a response; if no response, repeat the statement. Transmit the CASEVAC request information in the proper sequence. Ensure the transmission time is kept to a minimum (25 seconds maximum).

Line 1	Location of the extraction site; use grid coordinates with grid zone letters or latitude/longitude

It is not necessary to encrypt grid coordinates or latitude/longitude when using secure communications or field hospital equipment.

When using nonsecure communications, off-line encryption or authentication is required. To preclude any misunderstandings, state that grid zone letters (grid coordinates) are included in the message.

Off-line encryption or authentication is required so the evacuation asset crew not only knows where to pickup CAX, but also is able to plan the route if CAX must be extracted from more than one extraction site.

Line 2	Requesting unit's radio frequency and call sign/suffix

Send the frequency of the radio at the extraction site (this procedure will vector the aircraft/guide the ground vehicle); do not transmit the relay frequency.

The call signs (and suffix if used) of the person to be contacted at the extraction site may be transmitted in the clear. Obtain the radio frequency, call sign, and suffix from the signal operating instructions or the ANCD.

This information is required so the evacuation asset can contact the requesting unit while en route to obtain additional information (change in security level, vectoring, etc.).

Line 3	Number of casualties by precedence; use brevity codes

Report only applicable information and then use the appropriate brevity codes.

The brevity code precedes the description (A-Urgent).

Priority	Precedence	Brevity Code	Remarks
* Priority I	Urgent Complete	A	Evacuate as soon as possible or within two hours. Evacuation required to save life, limb, or eyesight and to avoid permanent disability.
* Priority IA	Urgent Surgical	B	Evacuate within two hours to the nearest (far-forward) surgical unit. Evacuation required to save life and stabilize for further evacuation.
* Priority II	Priority	C	Evacuate promptly or within four hours (or the medical condition could deteriorate to urgent).
* Priority III	Routine	D	Condition not expected to deteriorate significantly; evacuate within 24 hours.
* Priority IV	Convenience	E	Medical convenience rather than medical necessity**.

* Used for reference purposes.

** North Atlantic Treaty Organization Standardization Agreement 3204 has deleted this category; however, it is still included in U.S. Army evacuation priorities as there remains a battlefield requirement.

If two or more categories must be reported in the same request, insert the word "break" between each category.

This information is required by the unit controlling the evacuation asset(s) in order to assist in prioritizing missions when more than one mission is ongoing.

Line 4	Special equipment required; use brevity codes

Some types of equipment and their brevity codes are as follows:

Brevity Code	Item of Equipment	Remarks
A	None	
B	Hoist	If the air asset must extract the CAX while at a hover; a jungle penetrator and Stokes litter basket will be carried if the hoist is requested.
C	Extraction Equipment*	
D	Ventilator	

Information on special equipment requirements are determined as part of the evaluation of the CAX, mission, enemy, terrain and weather, troops and support available, time available, civil considerations and tactical situation.

This information is required so the equipment can be placed on the evacuation vehicle prior to the start of the mission.

* Combat search and rescue aircraft carry equipment designed to free CAX that remain trapped in vehicles or airframes.

Line 5	Number of casualties by type; use brevity codes

Report only applicable information.

If requesting evacuation for more than one type of casualty, insert the word "break" between the litter entry and ambulatory entry.

Brevity Code	Type Casualty	Remarks
L	Litter	(Litter) + number of CAX
A	Ambulatory	(Ambulatory) + number CAX

Information as to the type of CAX is obtained as part of the casualty evaluation process.

This information is required to determine the appropriate number of evacuation vehicles to be dispatched to the extraction site; the information is also needed to configure the vehicles to carry litter versus ambulatory versus a combination of the two.

Line 6	Security of extraction site; use brevity codes

This information is used during wartime.

Use one of the following brevity codes to transmit the information concerning the status of extraction site security:

Brevity Code		
N	No enemy (combatants) in the area	
P	Possibly enemy (combatants) in the area	Approach with caution
E	Confirmed enemy (combatants) in the area	Approach with caution
X	Engaged with enemy (combatants) in the area	Armed escort required

This information is required to assist the evacuation crew in assessing the situation and determining if assistance is required to accomplish the mission. More definitive guidance can be furnished to the evacuation vehicle while it is en route (for example, the specific location of the enemy assists the crew in planning the approach to the extraction site).

Line 7	Method of marking the extraction site; use brevity codes

Brevity Code	
A	Panels
B	Pyrotechnic signal
C	Smoke signal
D	None
E	Other

This information is based on the tactical situation and the availability of materials.

The information is required to assist the evacuation asset in identifying the specific location of the extraction site. The color of the panels, smoke, or other markings should not be transmitted until the evacuation vehicle contacts the unit just prior to arrival. For security reasons, the crew should identify the color of the marking(s), and the requesting unit should verify the color.

Line 8	Casualty nationality and status; use brevity codes

The brevity codes and categories are as follows:

Brevity Code	
A	U.S./Coalition military
B	U.S./Coalition civilian
C	Non-U.S./Coalition military
D	Non-U.S./Coalition civilian
E	* Enemy prisoner of war
F	* High value target

* Armed escort required if non-tactical aircraft/ground vehicle has been designated as the CASEVAC asset.

The number of CAX in each category need not be transmitted.

The information is required in planning for the destination of facilities and the need for guards.

The unit requesting the evacuation support should ensure there is an English-speaking representative at the extraction site.

Line 9	NBC contamination; use brevity codes

The brevity codes to indicate contamination are as follows:

Brevity Code	
N	Nuclear contamination present
B	Biological contamination present
C	Chemical contamination present

Include this line only when applicable.

This information is required to assist in planning for the mission, determining which evacuation vehicle will accomplish the mission, and when the mission will be accomplished (arrive at the extraction site). Information concerning the type of vehicle to be dispatched to the extraction site and the estimated time of arrival can be obtained from the evacuation unit.

Although not formally a part of the nine-line request, it is customary to transmit the nature of injuries, especially of potentially complex CAX.

Note: During peacetime, Line 6 (Security of extraction site) and Line 9 (NBC contamination) will change. Line 6 will become "Number and type of wound, injury, or illness" and Line 9 will become "Description of terrain."

Loading capacities:

Ground vehicles, ambulance:

Vehicle	Max Litter	Max Ambulatory
M996 Ambulance	2	6
M997 Ambulance	4	8
M1035 Ambulance	2	3
M1010 1¼-ton Tactical	4	8
M113 Carrier	4	10
M1133 Stryker Medical Evacuation Vehicle	6	3

Rotary-wing aircraft:

Aircraft	Max Litter	Max Ambulatory
UH-1H/V Iroquois	6	9
UH-60L Blackhawk	6	7
MH-60K/L Pave Hawk	4	11
CH-46 Sea Knight	15	25
CH-47 Chinook	24	31
MH-47D/E Chinook	24	33
CH-53 Sea Stallion	24	37
MH-53J/M Pave Low	14	20
V-22 Osprey	12	24

Fixed-wing aircraft:

Aircraft	Max Litter	Max Ambulatory
C-17 Globemaster III	36	54
C-130 Hercules	70	92
MC-130E Combat Talon I	12 (floor loaded)	32
MC-130H Combat Talon II	12 (floor loaded)	48
C-141B Starlifter	103	168
C-5B Galaxy	108	70
C-12 Huron	-	8
KC-135 Stratotanker	8	24
KC-10 Extender	8	24

Preparation of the extraction site (rotary-wing medical evacuation):

- Clear debris and mark any obstacles that cannot be removed.

- Provide sufficient space for rotary-wing to hover and maneuver during landing/takeoff.

- Secured VS-17 panels or beanbag lights to the ground, if appropriate.

- Mark pickup zone with the letter "H" or an inverted "Y," if the tactical situation permits.

Clearance diameter required:

UH-1	35 meters
UH-60	50 meters
CH-46, CH-47, CH-53, CH-54	80 meters

- Land aircraft into the wind if possible. Avoid landing on a down slope (more than 16 degrees)

- A special operations warfighter may guide (marshal) the aircraft using proper hand signals during landing and takeoff (tactical situation permitting).

- Prevent over classification (the tendency to classify a wound as more severe that it actually is).

- Use the order of precedence accurately.

- Keep transmissions 25 seconds or less.

- Ensure personnel loading the injured will take all commands regarding approach, loading, and unloading from the aircraft crew.

Relay requests: If the unit receiving the request does not control the evacuation means, it must relay the request to the headquarters or unit that has control of the evacuation assets or to another relaying unit.

When relaying to a unit without secure communications means:

- Transmit in encrypted form.

- Ensure the relayed information is exactly as originally received, regardless of the method of transmission.

- Ensure radio call sign and frequency relayed (Line 2) are that of the requesting unit and not that of the relaying unit.

- Monitor (intermediate headquarters or unit relaying the request) the frequency specified in Line 2, if possible.

Appendix C

Tactical Combat Casualty Care Form (New) (Field Medical Card)

Department of Defense/Health Affairs (HA) Force Health Protection asked the Tactical Combat Casualty Care (TCCC) Subcommittee on First Responders to look into the lack of information related to care rendered at the point of injury (POI) in the current conflict. To this point, with more than 30,000 wounded in action, less than 10 percent of records have any prehospital documentation; in only 1 percent of cases is the information available sufficient. "Home-grown" formats were used in almost all cases of successful documentation. Decision support, from Level IIB clinicians through HA leadership, requires this information to provide current and future guidance related to battlefield health care. Furthermore, in most instances, first responders are not medical personnel. Documentation of care provided by first responders must be in a format they can understand and use.

The Committee on Combat Casualty Care (CoTCCC) is uniquely positioned to provide this feedback due to its charter, expertise, membership, and system-wide implementation of TCCC guidelines. A special meeting was convened on 30 Aug 2007 to address this issue. This meeting included representation from the CoTCCC, as well as medics and physicians from all service components, including active and reserve components. Sixty individuals attended this conference and defined the environment of care under battlefield conditions. They also discussed the standard of care, realities of first responder documentation in the operational environment, and requirements for sufficient documentation of care provided. Currently, life saving interventions and other essential clinical data are not being captured for the longitudinal health care record. This procedure does not meet the TCCC standard of care because the institutional documentation tools, the paper form 1380 and the electronic Battlefield Medical Information System-Tactical, do not sufficiently meet the needs of the prehospital providers in the tactical environment.

This consortium outlined several key requirements to meet the standard of care for improved prehospital documentation (see attachments). Furthermore, the consortium decided on the minimum essential data elements to capture, which will ensure adequate transfer of vital information.

Services are not meeting TCCC standard of care (adopted by all services) because of the lack of information flow from POI to Level II. In order to meet that standard, certain critical elements of health care information must be communicated to insure optimal care; no current fielded solution exists. A new tool is needed to support TCCC at the POI. An immediate, cost-effective, and easily fielded interim solution that meets the TCCC standard of care is included in the attachments. CoTCCC will publish this form in the next edition of the Prehospital Trauma Life Support manual, and it will be posted on the TCCC Web site as an interim change.

Attachment 1

Criteria to build a successful TCCC tool:

- It works (evidenced based)

- Easy to apply/use

- Easy to train

- Rapid action (fast)

- Minimal complications (drug interaction/dose)

- Small packaging

- Long shelf life

- Environmental application (hot/cold/wet/dry/dark/light)

- Common accessories (battery, plug, etc.)

- Low cost

Concept of operations tenets:

- Minimum essential medical information recorded by first-responders:

   ° Is attached to and/or travels with the patient.

   ° Is visible and accessible to the flight/ambulance medic for en route care notes (run-sheet).

   ° Will remain with patients and be received/transmitted (read) and understood when they arrive at the combat support hospital (CSH) or forward surgical team.

- Location of elements needed by successive providers to assume responsibility for the patient.

- Minimum essential medical information accompanying patients in paper form is included in the patient's comprehensive record (electronic and paper).

- Theater CSHs start a paper medical chart/record on every patient admitted to the facility and new DD Form, TCCC be included. The form can be scanned and added to Armed Forces Health Longitudinal Technology Application-Emergency Medical Technician encounter.

- The DD Form, TCCC can also be harvested by trauma teams for relevant data elements:

   ° **Acute phase**: Casualty treatment documentation

                * Acute and blunt trauma information that needs to be conveyed during handover to the next provider.

                * Acute and detailed information that needs to be archived as an after-action review.

        ° **Casualty tracking**: From POI to home station

        ° **Chronic phase**: Long-term follow up and care and documentation:

                * Rehabilitation care

                * Convalescent care

                * Benefits and disability

Attachment 2

DD form, TCCC specifications:

- Two-sided form made of rigid, waterproof, tear-proof paper.

- Pre-attached cord or wire running through a grommet to ensure it can be attached to the patient and will not come off.

- Paper stock should be rigid and durable so that vitals, en route care, and medication can be scribed using the patient's body to support handwriting.

- Front side should be first responder information, and the back side should be a run sheet for evacuation crews.

- Card could be carried in a specified pocket of the Soldier's uniform; card would be pre-filled with demographics.

- Medics and evacuation crews can carry blank forms.

Requirements to meet goal of transmitting information regarding patient care rendered from POI to next level provider:

- Supports first-responder's tasks

- Must positively identify casualty

- Cannot detract from the mission and/or provider work

- Documentation of:

    ° Injury

    ° Treatment (TCCC)

- ° Time

- ° Physiologic status (lines of communication, airway, breathing, circulation, times, why intervention done)

- ° Medications (drugs, fluids, etc.)

- ° Vital signs (as obtainable)

- Format: pen/write (today)—verbal/visual for future? Prompted answers (closed-ended questions)

- Keep documentation with casualty

- Limit redundancy

Example of new DD form TCCC

Name/ID:		A: Intact Adjunct Cric Intubated
DTG:_____ALLERGIES:_____		B: Chest Seal NeedleD ChestTube
Friendly Unknown NBC		C: TQ Hemostatic Packed PressureDx

A: Intact   Adjunct   Cric   Intubated
B: Chest Seal   NeedleD   ChestTube
C: TQ   Hemostatic   Packed   PressureDx
   IV   IO

FLUIDS: NS / LR   500   1000 1500
   Hextend   500   1000
Other:

DRUGS (Type / Dose / Route):
PAIN
ABX
OTHER

TQ TIME

GSW BLAST MVA Other_____

TIME				
AVPU				
PULSE				
RESP				
BP				

DD FORM XXXX (Tactical Combat Casualty Care Card)

Medic's Name_____

Figure C-1

Appendix D
Acronyms Used in Handbook

ACLS	Advanced cardiac life support
ACS	American College of Surgeons
AMEDD	Army Medical Department
ANCD	Automated Net Control Device
A&O x	Alert and oriented (times orientation)
ATB	Antibiotic
ATLS	Advanced trauma life support
AVPU	Alert, verbal, pain, unresponsive
BIAD	Blind insertion airway device
BP	Blood pressure
BVM	Bag-valve-mask
C	Centigrade/Celsius
CASEVAC	Casualty evacuation
CAX	Casualties
CF	Conventional forces
CLS	Combat lifesaver
COT	Committee on Trauma
CoTCCC	Committee on Tactical Combat Casualty Care
CPR	Cardiopulmonary resuscitation
DCAP-BLS	Deformities, contusions, abrasions, penetrations, burns, lacerations, swelling
EBL	Estimated blood loss
ETC	Esophageal-Tracheal Combitube
ETT	Endotracheal tube
F	Fahrenheit
F.A.S.T.1	First Access for Shock and Trauma
FHP	Force health protection

FMC	Field medical card
FWB	Fresh whole blood
IED	Improvised explosive device
IM	Intramuscular
IO	Intraosseous
IV	Intravenous
kg	Kilogram
KIA	Killed in action
LOC	Level of consciousness; loss of consciousness
mcg	Microgram
MEDEVAC	Medical evacuation
mg	Milligram
ml	Milliliter
mmHg	Millimeters of mercury
MSO4	Morphine sulfate
MTF	Medical treatment facility
NBC	Nuclear, biological, and chemical
NPA	Nasopharyngeal airway
O^2	Oxygen
OEF	Operation Enduring Freedom
OIF	Operation Iraqi Freedom
OPA	Oropharyngeal airway
OPLAN	Operations plan
OPORD	Operations order
OTFC	Oral transmucosal fentanyl citrate
PASG	Pneumatic anti-shock garment
PHTLS	Prehospital trauma life support
PO	By mouth (Latin: *Per Os*)
POI	Point of injury

PRBC	Packed red blood cells
PTX	Pneumothorax
SEAL	Sea, Air, Land
SOF	Special operations forces
TBI	Traumatic brain injury
TCCC	Tactical combat casualty care
USAF	United States Air Force
USSOCOM	United States Special Operations Command
VBIED	Vehicle-borne improvised explosive device

Appendix E
References

Texts

Advanced Trauma Life Support for Doctors, 7th edition, American College of Surgeons, Mosby, 2004.

Basic and Advanced Prehospital Trauma Life Support: Military Edition, revised 6th edition, National Association of Emergency Medical Technicians, Mosby, 2006.

Emergency Medicine: A Comprehensive Study Guide, 6th edition, American College of Emergency Physicians, McGraw-Hill, 2004.

Emergency War Surgery, 3rd U.S. revision, Borden Institute, 2004.

Griffith's Five-Minute Clinical Consult, Lippincott, 2006.

Guidelines for Field Management of Combat-Related Head Trauma, Brain Trauma Foundation, 2005.

Prentice Hall Nurse's Drug Guide, Wilson, Shannon, and Stang, 2007.

Tactical Medical Emergency Protocols for Special Operations Advanced Tactical Practitioners (ATPs), U.S. Special Operations Command, 2006.

Tarascon Adult Emergency Pocketbook, 3rd edition, Tarascon, 2005.

Tarascon Pocket Pharmacopoeia, Tarascon, 2006.

The Sanford Guide to Antimicrobial Therapy, 35th edition, Antimicrobial Therapy, 2005.

Wilderness Medicine, 4th edition, Mosby, 2001.

Articles

R.F. Bellamy, "The Causes of Death in Conventional Land Warfare: Implications for Combat Casualty Care Research," *Military Medicine*, 149:55, 1984.

F.K. Butler, J. Hagmann, and E.G. Butler, "Tactical Combat Casualty Care in Special Operations," *Military Medicine*, 161(3 Suppl):1-15, 1996.

F.K. Butler, Jr., J.H. Hagmann, and D.T. Richards, "Tactical Management of Urban Warfare Casualties in Special Operations," *Military Medicine*, 165(4 Suppl):1-48, 2000.

J.B. Holcomb, "Fluid Resuscitation in Modern Combat Casualty Care: Lessons Learned from Somalia," *Journal of Trauma*, 54(5):46, 2003.

R.S. Kotwal, K.C. O'Connor, T.R. Johnson, D.S. Mosely, D.E. Meyer, and J.B. Holcomb, "A Novel Pain Management Strategy for Combat Casualty Care," *Annals of Emergency Medicine*, 44(2):121-7, 2004.

G.H. Lind, M.A. Marcus, S.L. Mears, et al., "Oral Transmucosal Fentanyl Citrate for Analgesia and Sedation in the Emergency Department,"*Annals of Emergency Medicine*, 20(10):1117-20, 1991.

C.K. Murray, D.R. Hospenthal, and J.B. Holcomb, "Antibiotic Use and Selection at the Point of Injury in Tactical Combat Casualty Care for Casualties with Penetrating Abdominal Injury, Shock, or Inability to Tolerate Oral Agents," *Journal of Special Operations Medicine*, 3(5):56-61, 2005.

K.C. O'Connor and F.K. Butler, "Antibiotics in Tactical Combat Casualty Care," *Military Medicine*, 168:911-4, 2003.

PROVIDE US YOUR INPUT

To help you access information quickly and efficiently, Center for Army Lessons Learned (CALL) posts all publications, along with numerous other useful products, on the CALL Web site. The CALL Web site is restricted to U.S. Government and allied personnel.

PROVIDE FEEDBACK OR REQUEST INFORMATION

<http://call.army.mil>

If you have any comments, suggestions, or requests for information (RFIs), use the following links on the CALL home page: "Request for Information or a CALL Product" or "Give Us Your Feedback."

PROVIDE TACTICS, TECHNIQUES, AND PROCEDURES (TTP) OR SUBMIT AN AFTER-ACTION REVIEW (AAR)

If your unit has identified lessons learned or TTP or would like to submit an AAR, please contact CALL using the following information:

Telephone: DSN 552-9569/9533; Commercial 913-684-9569/9533

Fax: DSN 552-4387; Commercial 913-684-4387

NIPR Email address: call.rfimanager@conus.army.mil

SIPR Email address: call.rfiagent@conus.army.smil.mil

Mailing Address: Center for Army Lessons Learned, ATTN: OCC, 10 Meade Ave., Bldg 50, Fort Leavenworth, KS 66027-1350.

TO REQUEST COPIES OF THIS PUBLICATION

If you would like copies of this publication, please submit your request at: <http://call.army.mil>. Use the "Request for Information or a CALL Product" link. Please fill in all the information, including your unit name and official military address. Please include building number and street for military posts.

CENTER FOR ARMY LESSONS LEARNED

CENTER FOR ARMY LESSONS LEARNED (CALL)

Access and download information from CALL's Web site. CALL also offers Web-based access to the CALL Archives. The CALL home page address is:

<http://call.army.mil>

CALL produces the following publications on a variety of subjects:

- **Combat Training Center Bulletins, Newsletters, and Trends**
- **Special Editions**
- *News From the Front*
- **Training Techniques**
- **Handbooks**
- **Initial Impressions Reports**

You may request these publications by using the "Request for Information or a CALL Product" link on the CALL home page.

COMBINED ARMS CENTER (CAC)
Additional Publications and Resources

The CAC home page address is:

<http://www.leavenworth.army.mil>

Battle Command Knowledge System (BCKS)

BCKS supports the online generation, application, management, and exploitation of Army knowledge to foster collaboration among Soldiers and units in order to share expertise and experience, facilitate leader development and intuitive decision making, and support the development of organizations and teams. Find BCKS at <http://usacac.army.mil/CAC/bcks/index.asp>.

Center for Army Leadership (CAL)

CAL plans and programs leadership instruction, doctrine, and research. CAL integrates and synchronizes the Professional Military Education Systems and Civilian Education System. Find CAL products at <http://usacac.army.mil/CAC/CAL/index.asp>.

Combat Studies Institute (CSI)

CSI is a military history "think tank" that produces timely and relevant military history and contemporary operational history. Find CSI products at <http://usacac.army.mil/CAC/csi/RandP/CSIpubs.asp>.

Combined Arms Center-Training: The Road to Deployment

This site provides brigade combat teams, divisions, and support brigades the latest road to deployment information. This site also includes U.S. Forces Command's latest training guidance and most current Battle Command Training Program COIN seminars. Find The Road to Deployment at <http://rtd.leavenworth.army.smil.mil>.

Combined Arms Doctrine Directorate (CADD)

CADD develops, writes, and updates Army doctrine at the corps and division level. Find the doctrinal publications at either the Army Publishing Directorate (APD) <http://www.usapa.army.mil> or the Reimer Digital Library <http://www.adtdl.army.mil>.

Foreign Military Studies Office (FMSO)

FMSO is a research and analysis center on Fort Leavenworth under the TRADOC G-2. FMSO manages and conducts analytical programs focused on emerging and asymmetric threats, regional military and security developments, and other issues that define evolving operational environments around the world. Find FMSO products at <http://fmso.leavenworth.army.mil/recent.htm> or <http://fmso.leavenworth.army.mil/products.htm>.

Military Review (MR)

MR is a refereed journal that provides a forum for original thought and debate on the art and science of land warfare and other issues of current interest to the U.S. Army and the Department of Defense. Find MR at <http://usacac.leavenworth.army.mil/CAC/milreview>.

TRADOC Intelligence Support Activity (TRISA)

TRISA is a field agency of the TRADOC G2 and a tenant organization on Fort Leavenworth. TRISA is responsible for the development of intelligence products to support the policy-making, training, combat development, models, and simulations arenas. Find TRISA Threats at <https://dcsint-threats.leavenworth.army.mil/default.aspx> (requires AKO password and ID).

United States Army Information Operations Proponent (USAIOP)

USAIOP is responsible for developing and documenting all IO requirements for doctrine, organization, training, materiel, leadership and education, personnel, and facilities; managing the eight personnel lifecycles for officers in the IO functional area; and coordinating and teaching the qualification course for information operations officers. Find USAIOP at <http://usacac.army.mil/CAC/usaiop.asp>.

Support CAC in the exchange of information by telling us about your successes so they may be shared and become Army successes.

Made in the USA
Coppell, TX
19 January 2020